Managing Editor
Ina Massler Levin, M.A.

Editor-in-Chief
Sharon Coan, M.S. Ed.

Contributing Editor
Mara Ellen Guckian

Cover Artist
Barb Lorseyedi

Art Coordinator
Kevin Barnes

Illustrator
Renee Christine Yates

Imaging
Ralph Olmedo, Jr.

Product Manager
Phil Garcia

Publishers
Rachelle Cracchiolo, M.S. Ed.
Mary Dupuy Smith, M.S. Ed.

Short Vowels

GRADES 1 & 2

Author

Lara L. Squires

Teacher Created Materials, Inc.
6421 Industry Way
Westminster, CA 92683

www.teachercreated.com

ISBN-7439-3335-4

©2002 Teacher Created Materials, Inc.
Made in U.S.A.

Table of Contents

Introduction

A good understanding of phonics is the foundation of a successful reading career for your child. The more practice and exposure your child has with phonics concepts being taught in school, the more success he or she is likely to find. For many parents, knowing how to help their child can be frustrating because they don't have the resources or knowledge of how best to help. This series has been written with the parent in mind. It has been designed to help parents reinforce basic skills with their children. Students should have an understanding of single consonant sounds prior to beginning the exercises in this book. Basic phonics skills involving short vowels will be reviewed for kindergarteners and first graders. The exercises in this book can be done sequentially or can be taken out of order, as needed.

The following standards or objectives will be met or reinforced by completing the practice pages included in this book. These standards and objectives are similar to the ones required by your state and school district. These standards and objectives are appropriate for kindergarteners and first graders.

- Match short-vowel sounds to appropriate letters.
- Read simple one-syllable words.
- Distinguish short-vowel sounds in single-syllable words.
- Create and state rhyming words with short vowel sound.
- Add, delete, or change target sounds in order to change words.

How to Make the Most of This Book

Here are some useful ideas for making the most of this book:

- Set aside a specific place in your home to work on this book. Keep it neat and tidy with materials ready.
- Set up a certain time of day to work on these practice pages to establish consistency, or look for times in your day or week that are less hectic and more conducive to practicing skills.
- Keep all practice sessions with your child positive and constructive. If the mood becomes frustrated or tense, set the book aside and look for another time to practice with your child. Forcing your child to perform will not help. Do not use this book as a punishment.
- Help beginning readers with instructions.
- Review the work your child has done and go over the answers together.
- Allow your child to use whatever writing instruments he or she prefers. For example, colored pencils can add variety and pleasure to drill work.
- Pay attention to the areas in which your child has the most difficulty. Provide extra guidance and exercises in those areas.
- Look for ways to make real-life application to the skills being reinforced. Play games with your child finding the vowel sounds in words. "Can you think of a word that begins with a *c* and has a short *a* sound?" CAT!

Introducing Short ă

When a word or syllable has only one vowel and it comes at the beginning of the word or between two consonants, the vowel makes a sound that is called "short." The sound the *a* makes in *cat* is the short *a* sound. Sometimes, we use a mark that looks like this (◡) over the *a* to show that a word has the short *a* sound.

The animals shown have the short *a* sound (yak, bat, cat, crab, alligator, ant). Color them.

Word Families

Add the letters at the top of each column to those to the side of the columns. Read all the short *a* words that are formed and learn to spell them.

at

b

fl

h

m

r

s

th

ad

b

d

gl

h

m

p

s

an

c

f

m

p

r

t

v

ap

c

cl

fl

l

m

n

t

Word Scramble

Unscramble these short *a* words. Write them correctly on the lines.

1. nam _____

2. rta _____

3. tca _____

4. apcl _____

5. tah _____

6. dal _____

7. rna _____

8. dap _____

Word Box

clap pad cat ran rat lad man hat

Practice

Read these short *a* words. Listen for the short *a* sound. Write the words three times.

1. bad

2. can

3. cap

4. fan

5. glad

6. lap

7. mad

8. sad

Draw faces to match these short *a* words.

bad	glad
mad	sad

Recognizing Words

Color each picture on the blanket. Then color the patches with the short *a* pictures red. Color the other patches blue.

8

Crossword Puzzle

Write the animal names in the crossword puzzle.

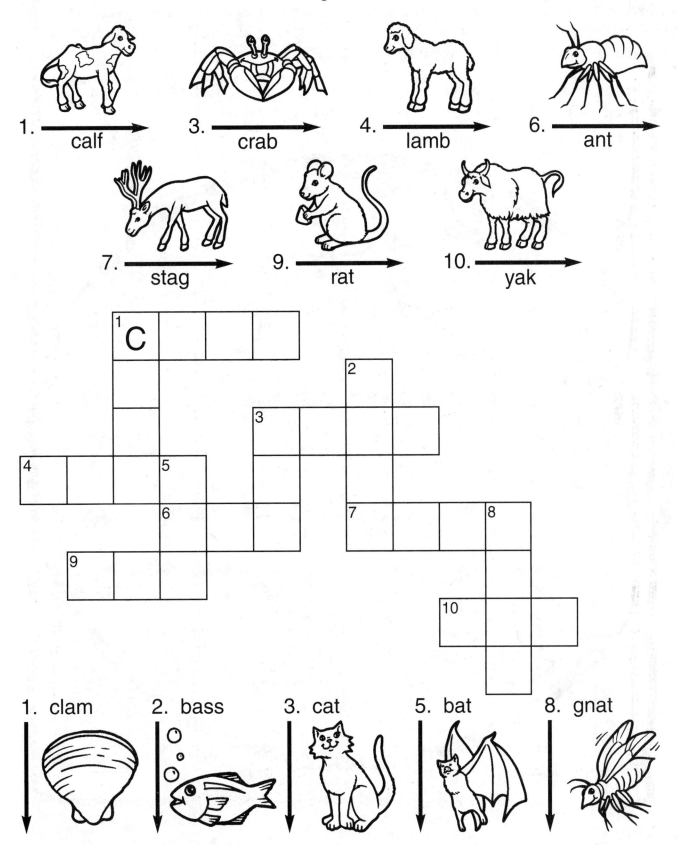

1. → calf   3. → crab   4. → lamb   6. → ant

7. → stag   9. → rat   10. → yak

1. clam   2. bass   3. cat   5. bat   8. gnat

Introducing Short ĕ

When a word or syllable has only one vowel and it comes at the beginning of the word or between two consonants, the vowel makes a sound that is called "short." The sound the *e* makes in *hen* is the short *e* sound. Sometimes, we use a mark that looks like (⏑) this over the *e* to show that a word has the short *e* sound.

The things shown here have the short *e* sound (elephant, hen, nest, vest, penguin, hedgehog). Color them.

10

Word Families

Add the letters at the top of each column to those to the side of the columns. Read all the short *e* words that are formed and learn to spell them.

et

g

j

m

n

p

v

w

est

b

p

r

t

v

w

z

en

B

d

h

m

p

th

wh

ell

b

c

f

s

t

w

y

Rhyming Words

Circle the pair of rhyming short *e* words on each nest. Color the picture.

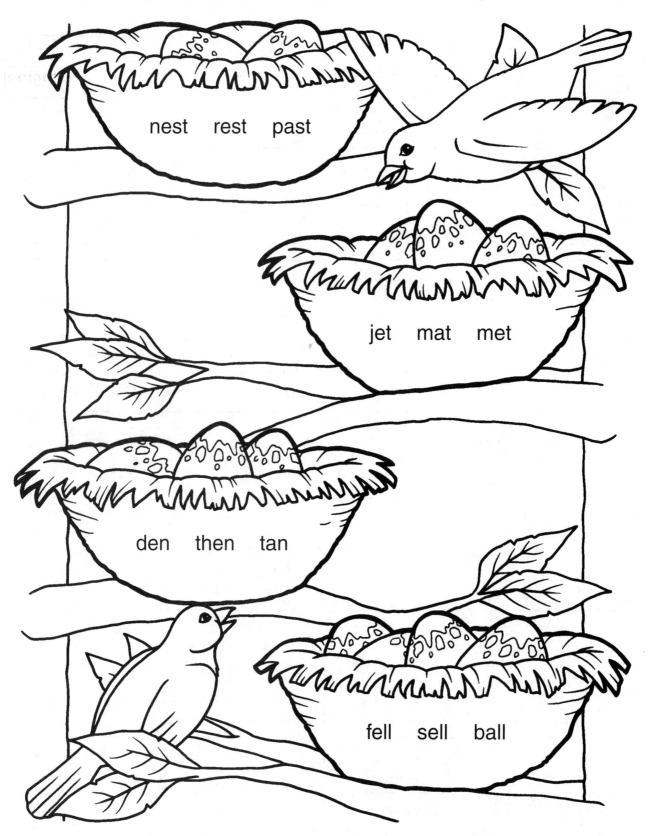

nest   rest   past

jet   mat   met

den   then   tan

fell   sell   ball

12

Secret Code

Look at the code. Write the letter in the blank above each number. Write the word on the line.

a	b	c	d	e	f	g	h	i	j	k	l	m	n	o	p	q	r	s	t	u	v	w	x	y	z
1	2	3	4	5	6	7	8	9	10	11	12	13	14	15	16	17	18	19	20	21	22	23	24	25	26

1. __ __ __
   23 5 20

2. __ __ __
   13 5 14

3. __ __ __ __
   26 5 19 20

4. __ __ __ __ __
   19 16 5 12 12

5. __ __ __
   13 5 20

6. __ __ __ __
   23 8 5 14

7. __ __ __ __
   20 5 12 12

8. __ __ __ __
   18 5 19 20

Completing Sentences

Read the sentences. Write the missing short *e* words in the blanks.

1. Ed _____ .

2. The _____ flew.

3. My _____ is a cat.

4. The man wore a _____ .

5. The bird flew to its _____ .

6. Can you _____ cat?

7. The lion lived in a _____ .

8. At _____ o'clock, we had a snack.

```
..................................................................
:                       Word Box                                 :
:   den          fell          jet          nest                 :
:   pet          spell         ten          vest                 :
..................................................................
```

Word Find

Circle the short *e* words in the puzzle. Words may go across or down.

b	e	l	l	h	v	f	g
c	h	w	h	e	n	g	e
p	x	g	t	v	r	c	t
e	p	n	l	k	j	s	v
n	k	j	p	j	e	x	c
v	e	s	t	s	t	l	g
s	p	e	l	l	f	n	q
g	n	b	p	v	h	e	n

Word Box

bell	hen	pen	vest
get	jet	spell	when

Introducing Short ĭ

When a word or syllable has only one vowel and it comes at the beginning of the word or between two consonants, the vowel makes a sound that is called "short." The sound the *i* makes in *pig* is the short *i* sound. Sometimes, we use a mark that looks like this (◡) over the *i* to show that a word has the short *i* sound.

The animals shown have the short *i* sound (pig, hippo, fish, iguana, cricket). Color them.

Word Families

Add the letters at the top of each column to those to the side of the columns. Read all the short *i* words that are formed and learn to spell them.

it

b _____

f _____

k _____

l _____

p _____

s _____

sl _____

ip

d _____

fl _____

h _____

l _____

r _____

sh _____

tr _____

in

b _____

ch _____

f _____

p _____

t _____

th _____

w _____

ill

b _____

f _____

h _____

m _____

p _____

s _____

st _____

Practice

Cut out the short *i* words. Paste them on the bubbles.

bat	gift	lip	pin
fin	hat	pig	ship

18

Completing Words

Finish each word with *it* or *in*.

1. b ___ ___

2. ch ___ ___

3. f ___ ___

4. h ___ ___

5. k ___ ___

6. p ___ ___

7. s ___ ___

8. th ___ ___

Finish each word with *ip* or *ill*.

1. b ___ ___ ___

2. h ___ ___ ___

3. h ___ ___

4. l ___ ___

5. m ___ ___ ___

6. p ___ ___ ___

7. r ___ ___

8. sh ___ ___

Word Scramble

Unscramble the letters to find out what short *i* gift is inside each box. Write the words on the lines. Draw pictures of the gifts on the boxes.

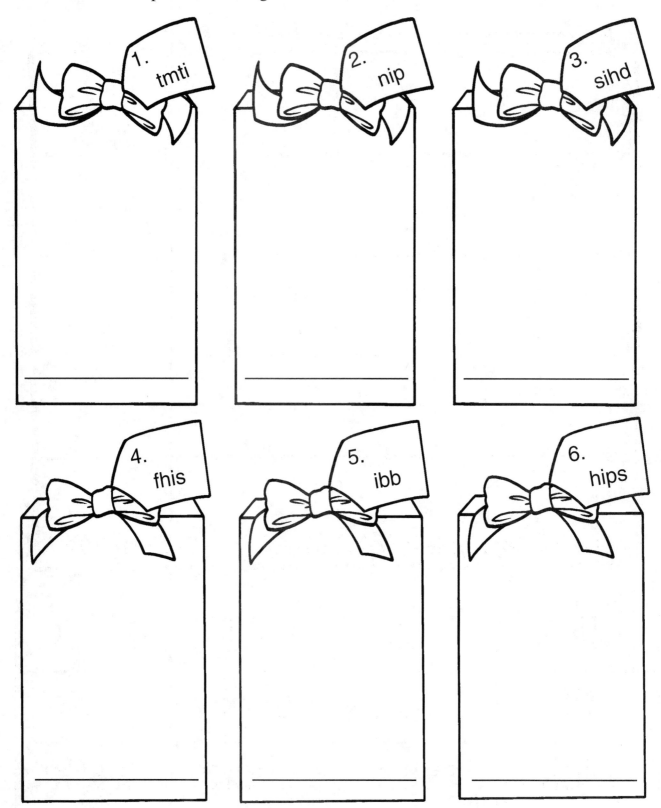

1. tmti

2. nip

3. sihd

4. fhis

5. ibb

6. hips

Rhyming Words

Cut out the bricks that have words that rhyme with *brick*. Paste them on the wall.
Learn to spell all ten words.

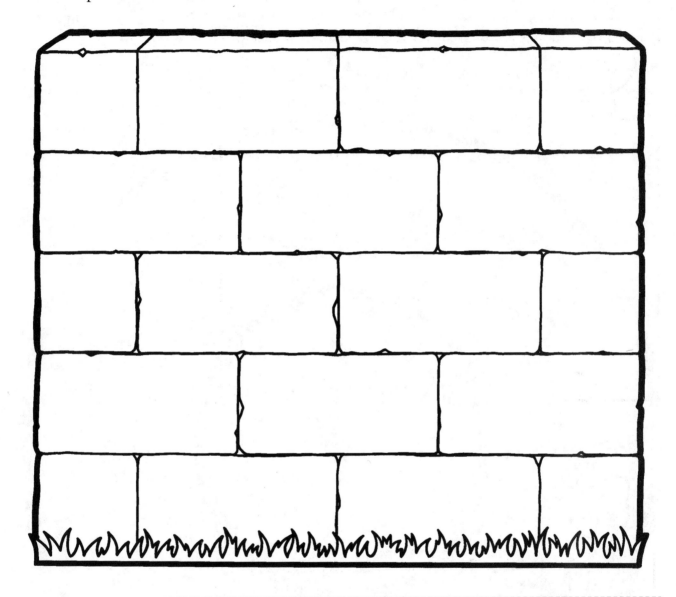

click	lick	rock	stick
fit	nick	sick	trick
kick	pick	slick	wick

Introducing Short ŏ

When a word or syllable has only one vowel and it comes at the beginning of the word or between two consonants, the vowel makes a sound that is called "short." The sound the *o* makes in *dog* is the short *o* sound. Sometimes, we use a mark that looks like this (◡) over the *o* to show that a word has a short *o* sound.

The animals shown have a short *o* sound (frog, ostrich, dog, fox, octopus, opossum). Color them.

Word Families

Add the letters at the top of each column to those to the side of the columns. Read all the short *o* words that are formed and learn to spell them.

op

dr _____

fl _____

h _____

m _____

p _____

pl _____

st _____

ock

bl _____

cl _____

d _____

kn _____

l _____

r _____

sh _____

ot

d _____

g _____

h _____

l _____

p _____

sp _____

tr _____

og

d _____

cl _____

f _____

fr _____

h _____

j _____

l _____

Crossword Puzzle Words

Fill in the crossword blocks with the correct short *o* words.

1.

5.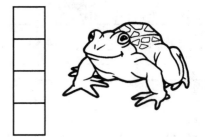

2.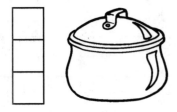

6.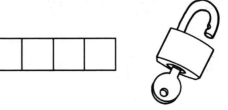

3.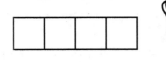

7.

4.

8.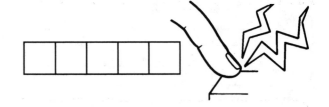

Word Box

clock	lock	mop	shock
frog	log	pot	sock

Word Find

Circle the short *o* words in the puzzle. The words may go across or down.

f	l	o	p	v	l	o	t
x	d	a	h	f	g	p	e
g	o	c	e	v	u	w	e
s	g	k	n	o	c	k	h
p	l	t	n	s	p	w	v
l	x	c	l	o	g	a	n
o	g	u	p	w	e	e	o
t	f	d	o	c	k	v	t

Word Box

dog	dock	knock	not
clog	flop	lot	plot

Completing the Word

Finish each word with *op* or *ot*. Color the pictures.

1. h ___ ___

2. h ___ ___

3. m ___ ___

4. p ___ ___

5. sp ___ ___

6. st ___ ___

7. t ___ ___

8. tr ___ ___

Finish each word with *ock* or *og*. Color the pictures.

1. cl ___ ___ ___

2. d ___ ___

3. d ___ ___ ___

4. fr ___ ___

5. h ___ ___

6. l ___ ___

7. r ___ ___

8. s ___ ___ ___

Completing the Sentence

Read the sentences. Write the missing short *o* words on the lines.

1. The bug hid under the _____ .

2. Bob drank _____ cocoa.

3. _____ at the red light.

4. The rabbit can _____ .

5. Dana went for a _____ .

6. The _____ is on top of the table.

7. My _____ likes to chew on a bone.

8. The _____ lives on the farm.

- -
Word Box

block	hog	hot	rock
dog	hop	jog	stop

Introducing Short ŭ

When a word or syllable has only one vowel and it comes at the beginning of the word or between two consonants, the vowel makes a sound that is called "short." The sound the *u* makes in *bug* is the short *u* sound. Sometimes, we use a mark that looks like this (◡) over the *u* to show that a word has the short *u* sound.

The animals shown have the short *u* sound (ladybug, butterfly, skunk, bunny, cub, duck). Color them.

28

Word Families

Add the letters at the top of each column to those to the side the columns. Read all the short *u* words that are formed and learn to spell them.

ug

b

d

h

j

m

r

t

um

b

g

gl

j—p

n—ber

s

t—my

uck

b

cl

d

l

st

t

tr

un

b

f

r

sp

ud

b

m

d

Identifying Words

Color the bugs that have words that rhyme with *bug*.

30

Word Find

Rearrange the letters on each bubble to spell short *u* words. Find and circle the words in the puzzle.

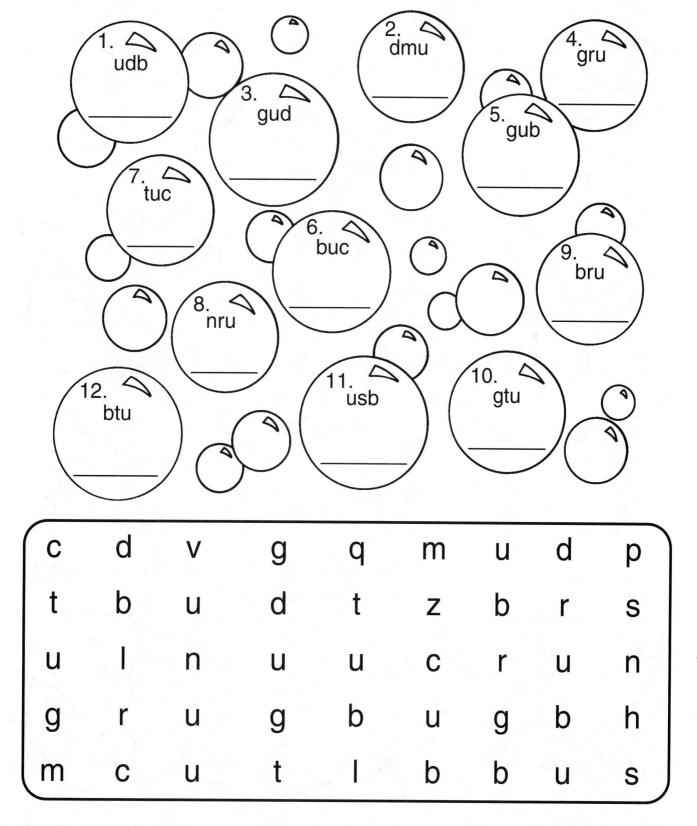

Rhyming Words

Color the gum balls that rhyme with *gum* blue.

Color the gum balls that rhyme with *rug* red.

Color the gum balls that rhyme with *cut* green.

Color the gum balls that rhyme with *sun* yellow.

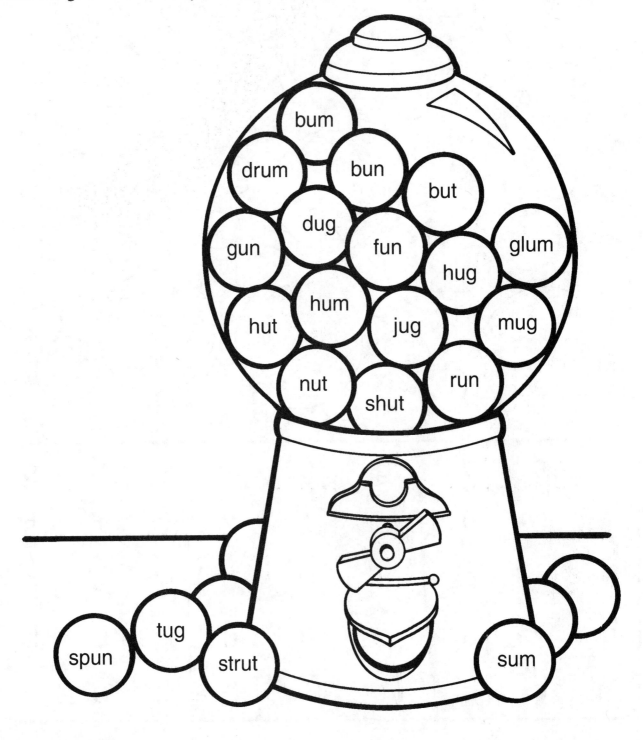

Crossword Puzzle Words

Fill in crossword blocks with correct short *u* words.

1.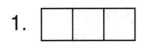

2.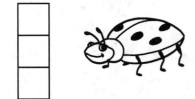

3.

4.

5.

6.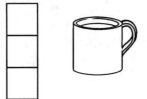

7.

8.

9.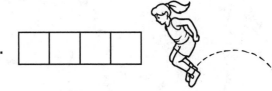

10.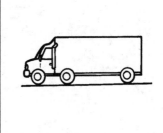

Word Box				
bud	bug	duck	gum	hug
jump	jug	mug	rug	truck

Identification

When a word or syllable has only one vowel and it comes at the beginning of the word or between two consonants, the vowel is usually short. How many pictures of short vowel words can you find in the picture? Color them.

34

Completing Words

To spell these short vowel words, fill in each blank with the correct vowel.

1. b ___ d

2. b ___ g

3. c ___ p

4. c ___ t

5. j ___ m

6. m ___ p

7. r ___ g

8. p ___ t

9. s ___ ck

10. s ___ ck

11. s ___ n

12. sp ___ n

Writing Words

Write the vowel you hear in each picture word. Read the short *a* words.

 1. _____	 2. _____	 3. _____	 4. _____
 5. _____	 6. _____	 7. _____	 8. _____
 9. _____	 10. _____	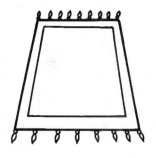 11. _____	 12. _____
 13. _____	 14. _____	 15. _____	 16. _____

36

Short ĕ and Short ŭ

Cut out the short *e* pictures and paste them on the top row. Cut out the short *u* pictures and paste them on the bottom row.

Short ĭ and Short ă

Color the pictures of words with the short *i* sound *red*.

Color the pictures of words with the short *a* sound *blue*.

 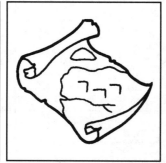 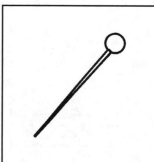 

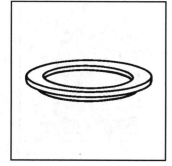   

Short ŏ and Short ŭ

Color the pictures of words with the short *o* sound *green*.

Color the pictures of words with the short *u* sound *purple*.

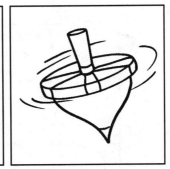

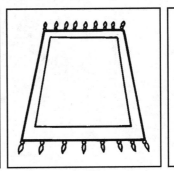

Mixed Practice

Fill in the missing letter in these short vowel words.

1. b ___ t	2. b ___ x	3. c ___ p
4. f ___ n	5. h ___ m	6. j ___ g
7. j ___ m	8. j ___ t	9. p ___ g
10. s ___ n	11. t ___ p	12. v ___ st

Mixed Practice

Fill in the missing letter in these short vowel words.

1.

b ___ g

2.

b ___ ll

3.

b ___ s

4.

d ___ g

5.

dr ___ p

6.

f ___ n

7.

g ___ m

8.

s ___ ck

9.

sw ___ m

10.

w ___ b

11.

___ x

12.

b ___ x

Mixed Practice

Fill in the missing letter in these short vowel words.

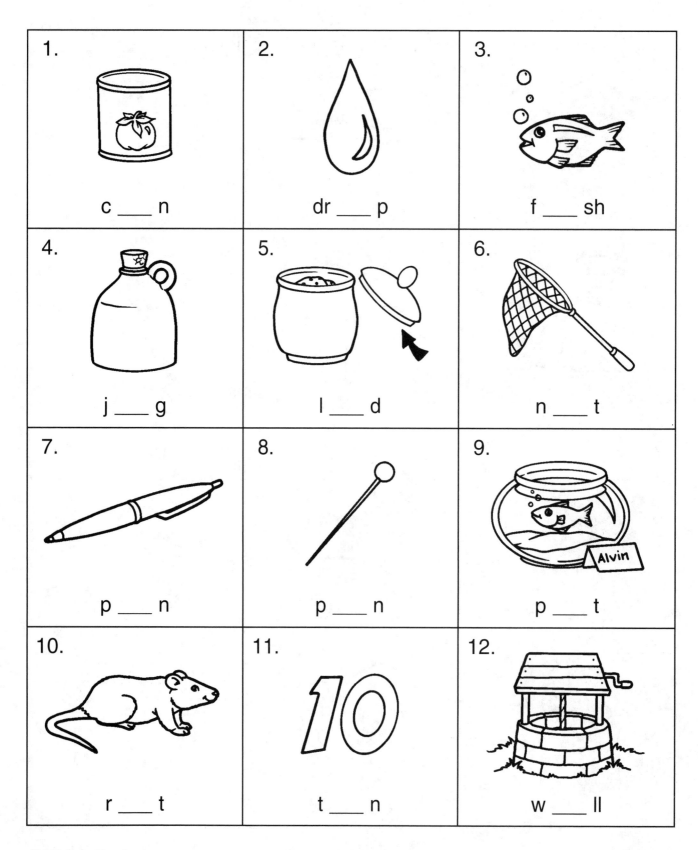

1. c ___ n	2. dr ___ p	3. f ___ sh
4. j ___ g	5. l ___ d	6. n ___ t
7. p ___ n	8. p ___ n	9. p ___ t
10. r ___ t	11. t ___ n	12. w ___ ll

42

Test Practice

1.

Which short vowel sound do you hear in this picture word?

○   ○   ○   ○   ○
a   e   i   o   u

2.

Which short vowel sound do you hear in this picture word?

○   ○   ○   ○   ○
a   e   i   o   u

3.

Which short vowel sound do you hear in this picture word?

○   ○   ○   ○   ○
a   e   i   o   u

4.

Which short vowel sound do you hear in this picture word?

○   ○   ○   ○   ○
a   e   i   o   u

5.

Which short vowel sound do you hear in this picture word?

○   ○   ○   ○   ○
a   e   i   o   u

Test Practice

Read the words from Word List 1. (Cover Word List 2.) Place a check mark (✓) by the words read correctly. Practice the unchecked words on the lines below. Repeat the process with Word List 2.

Word List 1		Word List 2	
1. bat	_____	1. pet	_____
2. met	_____	2. gum	_____
3. rest	_____	3. lid	_____
4. fit	_____	4. Sam	_____
5. kit	_____	5. rip	_____
6. cot	_____	6. test	_____
7. rat	_____	7. man	_____
8. rub	_____	8. dog	_____

Word Practice

Test Practice

Ask a parent or teacher to say the words on the Word Lists (page 44). Spell the words on the lines provided.

Word List 1

1. _____

2. _____

3. _____

4. _____

5. _____

6. _____

7. _____

8. _____

Word List 2

1. _____

2. _____

3. _____

4. _____

5. _____

6. _____

7. _____

8. _____

Test Practice

Fill in the circle under the picture that has the same short vowel sound as the picture in the box.

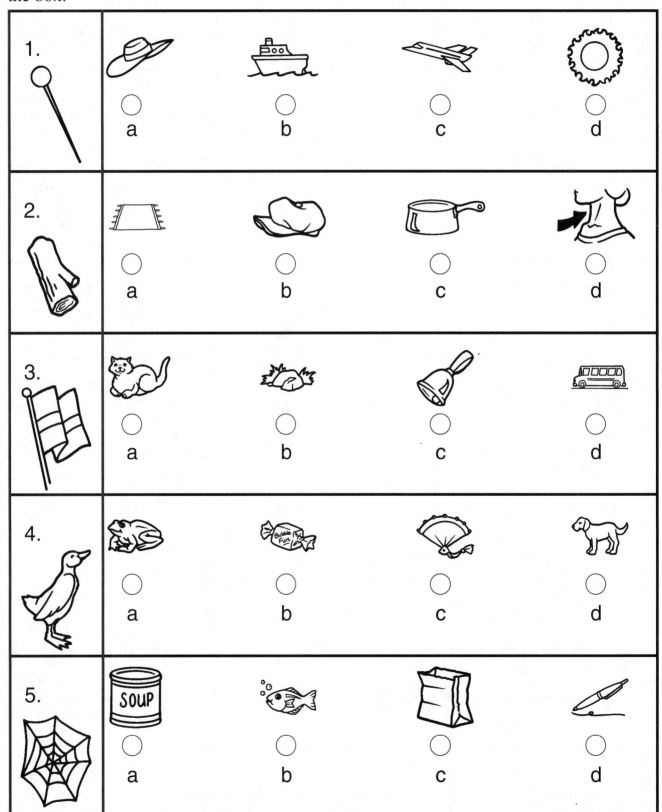

46

Answer Key

page 6
1. man
2. rat
3. cat
4. clap
5. hat
6. lad
7. ran
8. pad

page 9
1. calf
2. bass
3. cat (d) crab (a)
4. lamb
5. bat
6. ant
7. stag
8. gnat
9. rat
10. yak

page 12
nest, rest
jet, met
den, then
fell, sell

page 13
1. wet
2. men
3. zest
4. spell
5. met
6. when
7. tell
8. rest

page 14
1. fell
2. jet
3. pet
4. vest
5. nest
6. spell
7. den
8. ten

page 15
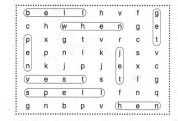

page 19
1. bit
2. chin
3. fin
4. hit
5. kit
6. pin
7. sit
8. thin

1. bill
2. hill
3. hip
4. lip
5. mill
6. pill
7. rip
8. ship

page 20
1. mitt
2. pin
3. dish
4. fish
5. bib
6. ship

page 24
1. log
2. pot
3. sock
4. clock
5. frog
6. lock
7. mop
8. shock

page 25
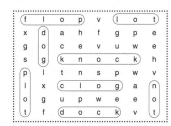

page 26
1. hot
2. hop
3. mop
4. pot
5. spot
6. stop
7. top
8. trot

1. clock
2. dog
3. dock
4. frog
5. hog
6. log
7. rock
8. sock

page 27
1. rock
2. hot
3. stop
4. hop
5. jog
6. block
7. dog
8. hog

page 30
dug, jug, hug, bug, rug,
snug, tug

page 31
1. bud
2. mud
3. dug
4. rug
5. bug
6. cub

7. cut
8. run
9. rub
10. tug
11. bus
12. tub

page 33
1. bud
2. bug
3. gum
4. hug
5. jug
6. mug
7. rug
8. duck
9. jump
10. truck

page 34
possible answers:
bat, opossum, sun, stag,
cub, ostrich, ox, hippo,
pig, fox, cat, duck,
lizard/iguana, fish,
alligator, penguin, skunk,
butterfly, frog

page 35
1. bud
2. bug
3. cap
4. cat
5. jam
6. mop

7. rug
8. pot
9. sick
10. sock
11. sun
12. spin

page 36
1. top
2. fish
3. ant
4. flag
5. sun
6. ship
7. jug
8. vest

9. dog
10. bell
11. rug
12. rock
13. cat
14. pig
15. bag
16. mug or
    cup

page 40
1. bat
2. box
3. cap
4. fin
5. hum
6. jog

7. jam
8. jet
9. pig
10. sun
11. top
12. vest

page 41
1. bug
2. bill
3. bus
4. dog
5. drip
6. fan

7. gum
8. sock
9. swim
10. web
11. ox
12. box

page 42
1. can
2. drop
3. fish
4. jug
5. lid
6. net
7. pen
8. pin
9. pet
10. rat
11. ten
12. well

page 43
1. a
2. u
3. i
4. e
5. o

page 46
1. b
2. c
3. a
4. b
5. d

Achievement Certificate

Fantastic News!

This is to report that

_____

has successfully completed

_____

Congratulations!

Date

48